T0031927

Climb, koala!

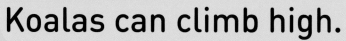

Koalas can climb high.

They spend a lot of time in trees.

Koalas have long, sharp claws.

The claws help them climb.

Koalas can sleep in trees, too.

Koalas can sleep for up to 18 hours a day!

They sleep almost all day.

When a koala wakes up,

Koalas need to eat a lot of leaves.

Sometimes they save them
in a pouch in their cheeks.

Koalas eat so many leaves, their fur smells like the leaves.

Their fur is warm. It keeps them dry in the rain.

Baby koalas aren't born with fur.

But their mom has a pouch.
It keeps them safe.

A baby koala is called a joey.

The baby lives in its mom's pouch.

It lives there for about
six months.

Then the baby climbs out.

Babies can ride on their mom's back or front.

It rides with its mom.

Baby koalas climb with their moms, too. Climb, koala!

Koalas and kids do some of the same things. What are these kids doing? Match the picture to the word.

EAT

SLEEP

RIDE

CLIMB

The publisher gratefully acknowledges the expert literacy review of this book by Kimberly Gillow, Principal, Milan Area Schools, Michigan.

Copyright © 2017 National Geographic Partners, LLC

Published by National Geographic Partners, LLC, Washington, D.C. 20036. All rights reserved. Reproduction in whole or in part without written permission of the publisher is prohibited.

Designed by Sanjida Rashid

Library of Congress Cataloging-in-Publication Data

Names: Szymanski, Jennifer, author.
Title: National Geographic readers. Climb, koala! / Jennifer Szymanski.
Description: Washington, DC : National Geographic, 2017. | Series: National Geographic readers | Audience: Ages 2 to 5. | Audience: Pre-school.
Identifiers: LCCN 2016041808 (print) | LCCN 2016055236 (ebook) | ISBN 9781426327841 (pbk. : alk. paper) | ISBN 9781426327858 (hard cover : alk. paper) | ISBN 9781426327865 () | ISBN 9781426327872
Subjects: LCSH: Koala--Juvenile literature.
Classification: LCC QL737.M384 S99 2017 (print) | LCC QL737.M384 (ebook) | DDC 599.2/5--dc23
LC record available at https://lccn.loc.gov/2016041808

Photo Credits
Cover, Suzi Eszterhas/Minden Pictures; 1 (CTR), Photographer/Kimball Stock; 2–3 (CTR), Jouan Rius/Minden Pictures; 4 (CTR), Greg Brave/Alamy Stock Photo; 6–7 (CTR), 1989_s/Getty Images; 8 (CTR), Tse Hon Ning/Getty Images; 9 (CTR), woodstock/Getty Images; 10–11 (CTR), Sidney Smith/Minden Pictures; 12 (CTR), Yva Momatiuk and John Eastcott/Minden Pictures; 13 (CTR), Freder/Getty Images; 14 (CTR), J & C Sohns/Getty Images; 15 (CTR), Cyril Ruoso/Biosphoto; 16–17 (CTR), Suzi Eszterhas/Minden Pictures; 18–19 (CTR), Suzi Eszterhas/Minden Pictures; 20 (CTR), Suzi Eszterhas/Minden Pictures; 21 (CTR), Constantin Stanciu/Alamy; 22 (CTR), Mitsuaki Iwago/Minden Pictures; 23 (UP), Cultura RM Exclusive/ Annie Engel/Getty Images; 23 (UP CTR), Tang Ming Tung/Getty Images; 23 (LO CTR), KidStock/Getty Images; 23 (LO), Caiaimage/Paul Bradbury/Getty Images; 24 (UP), Suzi Eszterhas/Minden Pictures

National Geographic supports K–12 educators with ELA Common Core Resources. Visit natgeoed.org /commoncore for more information.

Printed in the United States of America
22/WOR/4 (Paperback)
22/WOR/2 (RLB)

ANSWERS

EAT

SLEEP

RIDE

CLIMB

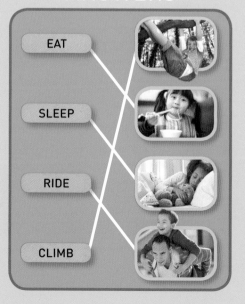